House of Commons

Environmental Audit Committee

GM Foods – Evaluating the Farm Scale Trials: the Government Response

Fifth Report of Session 2003–04

Report, together with formal minutes

*Ordered by The House of Commons
to be printed Tuesday 4 May 2004*

HC 564
Published on Monday 10 May 2004
by authority of the House of Commons
London: The Stationery Office Limited
£6.50

The Environmental Audit Committee

The Environmental Audit Committee is appointed by the House of Commons to consider to what extent the policies and programmes of government departments and non-departmental public bodies contribute to environmental protection and sustainable development; to audit their performance against such targets as may be set for them by Her Majesty's Ministers; and to report thereon to the House.

Current membership

Mr Peter Ainsworth MP (*Conservative, East Surrey*) (Chairman)
Mr Gregory Barker MP (*Conservative, Bexhill and Battle*)
Mr Harold Best MP (*Labour, Leeds North West*)
Mr Colin Challen MP (*Labour, Morley and Rothwell*)
Mr David Chaytor MP (*Labour, Bury North*)
Mrs Helen Clark MP (*Labour, Peterborough*)
Sue Doughty MP (*Liberal Democrat, Guildford*)
Mr Paul Flynn MP (*Labour, Newport West*)
Mr Mark Francois MP (*Conservative, Rayleigh*)
Mr John Horam MP (*Conservative, Orpington*)
Mr Jon Owen Jones MP (*Labour, Cardiff Central*)
Mr Elliot Morley MP (*Labour, Scunthorpe*)
Mr Malcolm Savidge MP (*Labour, Aberdeen North*)
Mr Simon Thomas MP (*Plaid Cymru, Ceredigion*)
Joan Walley MP (*Labour, Stoke-on-Trent North*)
David Wright MP (*Labour, Telford*)

Powers

The constitution and powers are set out in House of Commons Standing Orders, principally Standing Order No. 152A. These are available on the Internet via www.parliament.uk.

Publication

The Reports and evidence of the Committee are published by The Stationery Office by Order of the House. All publications of the Committee (including press notices) are on the Internet at: www.parliament.uk/parliamentary_committees/environmental_audit_committee.cfm.

A list of Reports of the Committee in the present Parliament is at the back of this volume.

Committee staff

The current staff of the Committee are: Mike Hennessy (Clerk); Eric Lewis (Committee Specialist); Elena Ares (Committee Specialist); Anna O'Rourke (Committee Assistant); Caroline McElwee (Secretary); and Robert Long (Senior Office Clerk).

Contacts

All correspondence should be addressed to The Clerk, Environmental Audit Committee, Committee Office, 7 Millbank, London SW1P 3JA. The telephone number for general inquiries is: 020 7219 6150; the Committee's e-mail address is: eacom@parliament.uk

References

In the footnotes of this Report, references to oral evidence are indicated by 'Q' followed by the question number. References to written evidence are indicated by page number as in 'Ev12'.

Contents

GM Foods – Evaluating the Farm Scale Trials: the Government Response

1. We published our Second Report of Session 2003-04, *GM Foods—Evaluating the Farm Scale Trials*, on Friday 5 March this year, a few days before the statement was made to the House on GM crops by the Secretary of State for Environment, Food and Rural Affairs, the Rt Hon Margaret Beckett MP[1]. We received the Government response to our Report on Wednesday 28 April, just four sitting days before the debate on the Floor of the House on GM Crops scheduled for Wednesday 5 May. This response appears as the Appendix to the Report.

2. We are very disappointed by the tone and content of the Government response. The Government claims to have given careful consideration to all available evidence. The few days between the publication of our Report and its statement on GM crops can simply not have allowed for careful consideration of the substantial amount of evidence contained within that Report and accompanying it. The debate scheduled for 5 May will not allow the House to come to a decision on the basis of a substantive, and amendable, motion.

3. The Government response is clearly unsatisfactory. It fails to reply to the substance of some arguments even while misinterpreting others. For example, the Government in its response suggests that our Report recommended that only for GM crops should the benchmark for biodiversity be raised. We clearly stated in our Report (paragraph 72) that "the Government…should establish a benchmark for conventional crops, at the less intensive end of the spectrum". This is only one of a number of either wilful or careless misinterpretations in the response to our Report that have permitted the Government simply to recapitulate old objections to the concerns raised by those who for good reason oppose the planting of GM crops in the United Kingdom.

4. The Government response tries to take us to task for its failure to take oral evidence from the research consortium engaged in the farm scale evaluations, a failure it regards as a "serious weakness". Yet it makes clear that it was the job of the Scientific Steering Committee (SSC), not the research consortium, to ensure that the design of the trials—with which we took greatest issue – was appropriate. We of course **did** take evidence from the Chairman of the SSC, and it was partly on the basis of that evidence that we came to the conclusions that we did. Given that, it is surprising that the Government came to such an insupportable conclusion. It is also unreasonable of the Government to criticise our report for placing undue emphasis on the North American experience when the Minister of State at DEFRA, Elliot Morley MP, in evidence before us maintained the need for DEFRA to examine the problems with GM in North America, and has indeed encouraged ACRE to look into the Canadian and US experience in some detail.

5. The Government response also fails to address the point that the farm scale evaluations (FSEs) reflected not only a narrow part of the assessment required under Directive 2001/18/EC but an even narrower part of the totality of the Government's consultation. Given that the conclusions of this thorough consultation were ambiguous or contradictory

---

1   HC Deb, 9 March 2004, cols 1381-4

when they were not negative, this is perhaps not surprising. It is, nonetheless, unsatisfactory.

6. The Government response does not address the issue of liability. It was clear from the statement of the Secretary of State on 9 March that the Government will not pay compensation for any contamination of conventional crops by GM crops. It is clear that the industry does not intend to do so either. It therefore appears that the Government is happy to leave conventional and organic farmers exposed to the possibility of severe financial losses and the GM industry free from mandatory inclusion in any scheme to establish proper liability.

7. We are grateful to the Government for asking ACRE to comment upon the issues raised by our Report and we look forward to reading its advice. We also commend the Government for its evident concern about what we have pointed out in our Report about the decline in biodiversity levels in conventional crops over previous decades. We further welcome the Government's intention to use its agricultural research programme to learn how different farming practices affect the environment at large. We however note that is unfortunate that such research has not already taken place and that harm to biodiversity has been permitted to take place unchecked for far too long.

8. We intend to return to the issue of GM crops later in the year when we will look at the issues raised by the Government response in more detail, and at the ever-growing body of evidence about the impact of GM crops on the environment. It is unfortunate that the Government has not responded in a more constructive way to our Report. The public at large are very concerned about issues relating to GM and will regard the Government's failure to engage in a proper debate with the Committee on this matter as a sign of weakness. We can only hope that the Government will show itself to be more open and responsive in the future.

Government Response

GOVERNMENT RESPONSE TO THE ENVIRONMENTAL AUDIT COMMITTEE REPORT: GM FOODS – EVALUATING THE FARM SCALE TRIALS. SECOND REPORT OF SESSION 2003-04

The Government welcomes this opportunity to respond to the Environmental Audit Committee's conclusions and recommendations regarding the value and relevance of the Farm Scale Evaluation GM crop trials (FSEs).

The Government continues to stand by the design and operation of the FSEs. They are the biggest ecological study ever undertaken on the effect of any farming practice, and are a credit to British science. The work has been internationally recognised and widely applauded. They produced robust and reliable data on the impact on biodiversity of the herbicide management of the GM crops in the trials. They have contributed to the consideration of our policy on GM crops, and our position on the particular crops in the trials. We await the results of the winter-sown oilseed rape FSE with interest

The EAC report was published on 5 March, a few days before the Government made its statement of policy on GM crops to Parliament on 9 March. The statement was not delayed, as requested by the EAC, because the report did not raise any new issues which would have justified such a delay. The Government's statement was the result of a long and painstaking assessment of GM crops. In deciding our policy we gave careful consideration to all the available evidence, including the reports from the GM public debate, science review and costs and benefits study, the AEBC report on co-existence and liability, as well as the results of the FSEs. Indeed no other country has undertaken such a comprehensive and rigorous assessment of the case for GM crops.

In our statement we have made it clear we would oppose applications to grow GM herbicide tolerant (GMHT) beet and spring sown oilseed rape commercially as managed under the regime in the FSEs. We also indicated we were prepared to agree in principle to the commercial growing of the GMHT maize subject to certain conditions, but in the light of the recent announcement by Bayer CropScience it is now clear that this particular variety of the crop will not be grown commercially in the UK.

We were surprised that the EAC conducted an inquiry evaluating the FSEs without talking to the research consortium that carried out the trials. In our view this was a serious weakness. By taking oral evidence from, and questioning, the researchers the Committee could have perhaps clarified some of the issues addressed in their report. This may have been particularly helpful in relation to issues such as the design of the trials, the measurement of yield, the follow up research on the withdrawal of atrazine and the involvement of the industry in the trials. It is surprising the Committee came to its conclusions without the benefit of expert advice from those directly involved.

The FSEs also raised important questions about the environmental impact of crop management practices as a whole and the need to find a balance between a competitive and economically viable farming industry and protecting our wildlife. Applying the lessons learned from the FSEs to assess and improve the impact of all forms of agriculture on the environment will be one of the most important tasks for Government to take forward out of this research.

We have asked our independent expert advisers, the Advisory Committee on Releases to the Environment (ACRE) to consider the range of issues that the EAC report has raised and it is expected to issue advice in due course.

In the text below the Committee's conclusions and recommendations are included in bold.

It is regrettable that the Government failed to be transparent about the nature of any deal made with the industry over the inclusion of beet. Given the public's concern and suspicion on matters relating to the GM industry we would expect greater openness. (Paragraph 25)

It is clear from the EAC's report that there was some confusion in the evidence provided by different sources and it is unfortunate that the EAC consider this reflects a lack of transparency on the Government's part. The agreement with the industry that led to the inclusion of the GMHT beet in the FSEs was made in November 1999, and announced and published at that time. This renewed the voluntary agreement between the Government and industry and expanded it to include other provisions in light of the experience of the pilot year for the FSEs.

When the FSEs were first proposed they were only intended to evaluate GMHT maize and oilseed rape, as these two crops were closest to commercialisation. An application for the beet was in progress, but was not as advanced. In designing the trials it was decided that a pilot year would be appropriate. On the basis that the GMHT beet crop was likely to have to undergo the same sort of process as the maize and the oilseed rape, the industry was keen for the beet to be included in this pilot year. It agreed to finance the trials in the pilot year for the beet crop on the same basis as the other crops. However, it did not, as suggested in the EAC report, offer to fund the entire FSE for the beet crop. Therefore, it is not the case that "the industry only accepted this toughened-up agreement on the basis that the Government takeover the funding the beet trials". We are not clear what evidence you have to make such a claim.

During the pilot year the beet application advanced through the regulatory process to the point where it became appropriate to reconsider its inclusion in the FSEs and the Government agreed to do this in the November 1999 agreement. Subsequently it was confirmed that beet would be included in the FSEs on the same terms as the maize and oilseed rape.

We consider it unfortunate that, as there was no definite yield component to the results of the FSEs, rumours and assertions have been allowed to proliferate concerning how the crops performed. (Paragraph 41)

We expect future trials to incorporate robust protocols for formal measurements of yield. (Paragraph 41)

Measurements of yield were not included as part of the FSEs as they were not necessary for the purposes of the research. The researchers, in consultation with Scientific Steering Committee (SSC), chose instead to take a variety of measurements of the growth stage of the crop. This approach was considered a more reliable indicator of the performance of the crop under its respective herbicide management throughout its growth. The detail included in the FSE results (the paper by *Champion et al*) of the manner in which the management of the crop was audited, and the close similarity of the growth patterns of all three crops provide convincing evidence that the herbicide management regimes reflected 'cost effective weed control'.

Even if measurements of yield had been included it does not follow that this would have provided the conclusive evidence the Committee desires. Farmers in the FSEs were free to choose the conventional varieties that they grew alongside the GM crop according to their experience and local conditions. Yield comparisons would not be useful in this context because of the wide variability in yield between conventional varieties. For example, for maize in 2002 the range across the national list was 12.9 to 17.1 t/ha dry matter yield. A further complication for both maize and beet was that the time of harvest was brought forward to a date earlier than would be usual for the GMHT varieties, in order to meet the conditions of the consent regarding the need to avoid material entering the human food chain. Therefore, for maize and beet at least, the GMHT yields could not have been compared fairly with varieties in current commercial practice.

It was not the purpose of the FSE trials to assess the yield performance of GMHT crops, and the requirements for any future trials will be determined by what is appropriate to assess the issue being researched. We will not insist that measurements of yield are included regardless. As noted in the EAC report yield is one of the factors assessed when considering seed varieties value for cultivation and use as part of the National Seed Listing process. Farmers make commercial decisions about which crop varieties to grow, and the presumption must be that they will grow the variety that is most beneficial for them. Yield may or may not be the determining factor in their decision but that is a commercial matter.

In the context of public concern about GM crops and the North American experience with GM, we believe that in order to determine the cumulative effect of rotational crops upon biodiversity, the FSEs for those crops should have lasted longer than three years. The trials on forage maize should also have lasted longer. We believe that the Government must take account of this in any future trials. (Paragraph 46)

The SSC overseeing the evaluations was satisfied that the design of the trials was appropriate. The crops in the evaluations are generally grown for one year as break crops in arable rotations. The size and scale of the evaluations was chosen to give sufficient power to test the hypothesis. On the basis of the results, the researchers were confident that in the case of rape and beet the effects seen after one year would have a cumulative adverse effect over subsequent years. In the case of maize the effects after one year indicated beneficial cumulative effects. This view was endorsed by the SSC and by ACRE. Therefore the hypothesis was rejected in each case and conducting additional trials in subsequent years would not add anything.

If the crops were to be grown commercially they would be subject to monitoring based on the environmental risk assessment submitted with the application. If evidence were to come to light from this monitoring that called into question the FSE results, or any other aspect of the environmental risk assessment, then the approval would be reassessed. It is also worth noting that consents issued for GM crops are time-limited. The consent holder must submit another application to renew this consent. This would have to include the results of any monitoring, and any other new evidence that has become available.

We are concerned that the GMHT forage maize trials were based on an unsatisfactory, indeed invalid, comparison. It is vital that the Government permit no commercial planting of GMHT forage maize until that crop is thoroughly re-trialled against a non-GM equivalent grown without the use of atrazine. (Paragraph 50)

It is clearly unsatisfactory that no definite statement has yet been made as to what the results were from the 25% of conventional forage maize fields in which atrazine was not used and whether or not this sample constitutes a large enough base from which to extrapolate comparable results for non atrazine conventional maize against GMHT maize. (Paragraph 51)

We do not accept that the maize trial was based on an unsatisfactory or invalid comparison. Within the period of the trials the use of atrazine was the predominant method of herbicide management on conventional maize and it was entirely appropriate that its use was permitted during the FSEs. The range of approved herbicides is often subject to change. Over the course of any long-term study there is a high probability of such changes, and withdrawals occurred during the FSE for the chemicals bromoxynil and avadex, used respectively on spring oilseed rape and beet. The EU decision to phase out atrazine (and other triazines) was not taken until a year after the spring sown FSE trials were complete and will not take full effect until autumn 2005. It is also important to emphasise that atrazine is being phased out not because of its effectiveness for weed control, but because of the risk of unacceptable contamination of groundwater. Future conventional herbicide regimes that replace atrazine could have equivalent, or even greater, impacts on weed populations.

We do not accept that there is a need for the GMHT maize to be retrialled. It is the herbicide management of conventional maize that will be changing as a result of the phasing out of atrazine, not the GM maize. Further trials on the GM maize would not tell us anything new about the impact of the herbicide management of the crop on biodiversity, and thus would not be an appropriate use of taxpayers' money. We made clear that if the consent holders were to seek to renew the existing consent for the GM maize when it expires in 2006 they would need to submit new evidence providing a comparison against conventional practice current at that time.

A peer-reviewed analysis of the impact on the maize FSE results of the phasing out of atrazine by members of the FSE research consortium (Perry et al) was published by *Nature* on 4 March. This concluded that the benefits to biodiversity of growing GMHT maize compared to conventional maize would be reduced but not eliminated by the withdrawal of atrazine. This suggests that in the short-term the banning of atrazine will not invalidate the conclusions of the FSE with respect to GM maize.

The problems in North America have not been taken seriously enough. Defra should have advised the SSC to take account of North American experiences with GM. (Paragraph 31)

We are unhappy that this work on north American GM experiences has been left until after most of the FSEs have reported. Consequently, the findings from that trans-Atlantic research have not now been factored in to the decisions that are already being reached on those GMHT crops in the UK nearest approval. This is clearly unsatisfactory. No decision to proceed with the commercial growing of GM crops should be made until thorough research into the experience with GM crops in North America has been completed and published. (Paragraph 31)

The North American experience with oilseed rape and the devastation of organic rape production should serve as an impetus to Government to bring in prudent guidelines for separation distances as quickly as possible. (Paragraph 37)

We are very concerned about possible contamination by gene-flow and pollen spread of non-GM crops and insist that the issue of liability be settled before any GM crops are allowed to be commercially grown in the UK. The Government should ensure, through primary legislation, if necessary, that it puts in place, before any GM crops may be grown commercially in this country, a clear and comprehensive liability regime to underpin any future regulations dealing with co-existence issues. Moreover, liability should lie with the industry and not with farmers. It would be wrong for the Government to allow farmers to be used as a firewall for the industry. (Paragraph 38)

Any evidence from North America that is relevant to the safety assessment of GM crops in the UK is always considered very carefully. However, the FSEs were focused on a specific issue. The general experience of commercial GM cropping in North America is of more relevance to a wider discussion about GM crops rather the conduct of a specific research project. In addition it is a valid argument that agronomic conditions differ significantly between the UK and the US. For example different climates, weed populations, and the fact that maize in the US is typically cultivated for grain production whereas in the UK it is typically a fodder crop.

There has been contradictory information coming out of North America on the performance of GM crops. In our view the EAC's assessment of the experience of GM crops in North America is unduly negative. In particular we are surprised at the prominence given to the views of the Canadian National Farmers Union given that we understand that they represent less than 3% of farmers in Canada. A cross section of views would have helped come to a balanced conclusion. If it turns out that a crop ceases to offer farmers any tangible benefit then the presumption must be that they will stop growing it. However, the use of GM crops in Canada and the USA continues to increase, and increased again last year. For example GM varieties accounted for 40% and 58% of US and

Canadian maize, and 84% and 68% of the respective oilseed rape crops, in 2003. This would suggest that the majority of farmers growing GM crops in North America see commercial benefits.

We accept that there are issues that have been raised in the context of the experience in North America that have to be addressed, but these are separate from the FSE research. For example, to the extent that there have been contamination problems in North America, this may reflect the fact that few, if any, steps have been taken there to manage the co-existence of GM and non-GM crops. As we made clear in our policy statement we intend that co-existence measures will be in place here before any commercial GM crops are sown. Our intention is that GM producers should observe a code of practice on co-existence with statutory backing, based on the 0.9% EU labelling threshold for adventitious GM presence. We will consult on this, on whether a lower GM threshold might apply for organic production, and on options for compensating non-GM farmers who suffer financially because a GM presence exceeds statutory thresholds.

We are concerned that the industry was responsible for a number of key inputs into the operation of the trials which appear to have been assessed only against very broad or vague criteria, or which were taken on trust. Even if these inputs had no cumulative effect upon the results, they were significantly integral to raise significant concerns as to the extent to which the industry was in practice capable of influencing the trials. (Paragraph 62)

It was the industry body SCIMAC which provided the inputs to the evaluations. SCIMAC is an umbrella body comprising UK Agricultural Supply Trade Association, National Farmers Union, Crop Protection Association, British Society of Plant Breeders and British Sugar Beet Seed Producers Association. As the EAC report itself acknowledges there were various inputs into the operation of the FSEs that it was entirely appropriate for the industry to provide, and indeed the trials could not have taken place without this degree of industry involvement. There is no substantiated evidence to support the concern that the industry may have unduly influenced the trial results. The research consortium audited the management of the trials and concluded that there was no evidence of bias in the inputs into the trials (See *Champion et al*).

Damage to the trial sites should be seen by those responsible for that damage as counterproductive, since it undermines the scientific validity of evidence that could well support their claims. We support the lawful right to protest but feel that future trials should be better protected in order to safeguard scientific evidence that may prove very valuable in domestic and international discussions as to whether the commercial growing of GM crops should proceed. Defra must consult with appropriate security bodies about achieving more secure trials in future. (Paragraph 57)

We share the Committee's concern about damage to trial sites. The Government and the industry put significant effort into protecting the FSE sites. The Government is committed to the principle of transparency and as such we made all locations of sites public, and made information explaining the trials available to people and farmers close to the crop trials. We also liased with the police, and ensured they were fully informed. We understand that in some cases the industry provided private security for farmers, their families and their property at certain times in response to threats and intimidation. However, it was simply not feasible to provide this at all the FSE sites for the duration of the trials.

It is unfortunate that a small number of saboteurs have abused our policy of publishing detailed site locations. But the actions of these extremists have not lessened our commitment to transparency, particularly the need to provide adequate information to people and farmers close to GM crop trials. We appreciate the concern that a legitimate activity is being hindered and we are keeping our policy on site disclosure under close review. However, it is difficult to see, without devoting disproportionate resources to the task, what can practically be done to increase protection of the trial sites.

It is vital the Government makes clear in its decision exactly what will be required of applicants in future, and how it will assess whether there is evidence of biodiversity harm from the use of the GM crop and herbicide regime for which the particular application is made. (Paragraph 65)

We agree that the industry should pay for any future trials including the future trials we think necessary for forage maize. (Paragraph 65)

We recommend that future GM crop assessments of biodiversity impact should be no shorter than four years. (Paragraph 67)

We expect to see thorough multi-year and multi-site trials for any new applications. We likewise expect comparative assessment of biodiversity harm to be undertaken on a crop-by-crop basis. (Paragraph 68)

ACRE has carefully considered what will be required of future applicants seeking to market GM crops in the UK in terms of wider biodiversity risk assessment. ACRE established a sub-group in 1999 specifically to address this question, full details of this 'ACRE sub-group on wider biodiversity issues' are available on its website[2], including minutes of its meetings.

The sub-group published a guidance document in July 2001[3]. This guidance reinforces the need for case-by-case assessment of crop management effects. It is conceivable that some potential crop management systems might differ little from existing practice while others may present novel systems of which there is little previous experience. One may require little or no field testing while another might require years of testing and/or monitoring. It would not be appropriate to be prescriptive about the level and duration of testing required. One of the most notable factors in the FSE results was the consistency of the treatment effects over many independent variables, including years. This suggests that trials of this scale and length are unlikely to be necessary in the future.

It is clear from Directive 2001/18/EC that the onus is on the applicant to undertake such trials as are considered necessary to provide the level of evidence required by the regulatory authorities. This was not the case under the preceding Directive 90/220/EEC. The detailed design of any future trials will need to be decided on a case-by-case basis.

---

2   www.defra.gov.uk/environment/acre/biodiversity/index.htm

3   www.defra.gov.uk/environment/acre/biodiversity/guidance/index.htm.

The benchmark against which GMHT crops were measured was not ambitious, since biodiversity in conventional crops has suffered greatly over the last half-century. (Paragraph 6)

Biodiversity levels have slipped intolerably over the last fifty years and Government has a duty to attempt to regain some of that lost ground. Indeed, the Government, in the light of the Curry report, should establish a benchmark for biodiversity in conventional crops, at the less intensive end of the spectrum. It is against this benchmark that future trials should assess innovatory practices and regimes in conventional agriculture. This ought to make the benchmark used in the FSEs irrelevant. (Paragraph 72)

While we applaud the steps the Government has taken to assess biodiversity in a rational way before permitting an agricultural innovation in the form of GM, we believe that even if some GM crops with some associated herbicide regimes are eventually shown to be less harmful to biodiversity than their conventional counterparts, the Government and its advisory bodies are still guilty of setting too low the level of harm. (Paragraph 73)

We therefore recommend that in future trials the biodiversity benchmark against which GM crops should be assessed should be that associated with the less intensive and more biodiversity-friendly end of the spectrum found in UK agriculture, such as organic crops. (Paragraph 73)

We share the EAC's concern that biodiversity levels have suffered over previous decades. However, in the specific case of the FSEs we do not accept that the 'benchmark' should have been set at a higher level. The FSEs must be placed in their regulatory context. The indirect environmental impact of the management techniques associated with GM crops compared to the management of the non-GM counterpart is one aspect of the risk assessment of a GM crop required by Directive 2001/18/EC. The key comparison, in order to make regulatory decisions, was thus an assessment of the herbicide management of the GMHT crop against the current herbicide management of its conventional counterpart. Some conventional crops performed poorly in relation to biodiversity in relation to the chemical inputs. It is not clear why even when the Committee accepts some GM crops may be less harmful to biodiversity they alone must pass a threshold not applied to conventional ones.

The FSEs also raised important questions about the environmental impact of crop management practices as a whole and our strategy for sustainable farming. The trial crop with the 'best' results for the environment was a conventional crop and the one which was 'worst' was also a conventional crop.

We are looking carefully at how the experience of the evaluations can help us to strike the appropriate balance between the needs of an economically healthy and competitive farming sector and the need to protect our wildlife. This will include a consideration of what is the most appropriate 'benchmark' against which crops and management systems should be assessed. The FSEs are invaluable in informing our consideration of such a benchmark as the studies are the most thorough assessment of any crop management systems ever undertaken. The FSE results in particular will contribute to the development of the Sustainable Farming and Food Strategy which incorporates our objectives to increase biodiversity in farmland and also will inform the development of the England Biodiversity Strategy and future agri-environment and cross-compliance schemes.

In addition we intend to see how the methodology used in the FSEs can be streamlined and improved to be less resource intensive, and will consider how a similar approach may be more widely applied to assess the risks of other (non-GM) crop or farm management situations, such as pesticides or the introduction of new bio-fuel crops or to assess the true value of organic systems. In our agricultural research programme we will apply the lessons learned about how different farming practices interact and how these in turn affect the environment at a landscape scale.

It is inconceivable that beet or spring sown oilseed rape will be given consents to be grown if managed under the same regime as applied in the FSEs. (Paragraph 63)

The scope of the trials was very narrow and the results cannot be regarded as adequate grounds for a decision to be taken in favour of commercialisation (Paragraph 74)

It would be irresponsible for the Government to permit the commercialisation of GM crops on the basis of one narrow component of the entire evaluation of GM technology. This would be the case even were there no significant doubts about as to the robustness, validity and relevance of the FSE results. (Paragraph 75)

The FSE trials were designed to address the specific question of the impact on biodiversity of the herbicide management regimes associated with GM crops. They addressed only one aspect of the required risk assessment and on their own they were never intended to be the sole basis for a decision to commercialise GM crops. When considering applications the full range of safety issues required for the risk assessment will be considered, as specified in Directive 2001/18/EC.

The Government's policy statement made it clear we would oppose applications to grow GMHT beet and spring sown oilseed rape commercially as managed under the regime in the FSEs.

Department for Environment, Food and Rural Affairs

April 2004

Formal minutes

Tuesday 4 May 2004

Members present:
Mr Peter Ainsworth, in the Chair

Mr Gregory Barker	Mr Paul Flynn
Mr Colin Challen	Mr Mark Francois
Mrs Helen Clark	Joan Walley
Sue Doughty	Mr David Wright

The Committee deliberated.

Draft Report (GM Food – Evaluating the Farm Scale Trials: the Government Response), proposed by the Chairman, brought up and read.

Ordered, That the Chairman's draft Report be read a second time, paragraph by paragraph.

Paragraphs 1 to 8 read and agreed to.

Resolved, That the Report be the Fifth Report of the Committee to the House.

Ordered, That the Chairman do make the Report to the House.

[Adjourned till Wednesday 5 May at 3pm.

Past reports from the Environmental Audit Committee since 1997

2003-04 Session

First   Annual Report 2003, HC 214
Second   GM Foods – Evaluating the Farm Scale Trials, HC 90
Third   Pre-Budget Report 2003: Aviation follow-up, HC 233
Fourth   Water: The Periodic Review 2004 and the Environmental
     Programme, HC 416
Fifth   GM Foods – Evaluating the Farm Scale Trials, HC 564

2002-03 Session

First   Pesticides: The Voluntary Initiative, HC100 (*Reply, HC 443*)
Second   Johannesburg and Back: The World Summit on Sustainable
     Development–Committee delegation report on proceedings, HC 169
Third   Annual Report, HC 262
Fourth   Pre-Budget 2002, HC 167 (*Reply, HC 688*)
Fifth   Waste – An Audit, HC 99 (*Reply, HC 1081*)
Sixth   Buying Time for Forests: Timber Trade and Public Procurement -
     The Government Response, HC 909
Seventh   Export Credits Guarantee Department and Sustainable
     Development, HC 689 (*Reply, HC 1238*)
Eighth   Energy White Paper – Empowering Change?, HC 618
Ninth   Budget 2003 and Aviation, HC 672 (Reply, Cm 6063)
Tenth   Learning the Sustainability Lesson, HC 472 (*Reply, HC 1221*)
Eleventh   Sustainable Development Headline Indicators, HC 1080 (*Reply,
HC 320)*
Twelfth   World Summit for Sustainable Development – From rhetoric to
     reality, HC 98 (*Reply, HC 232*)
Thirteenth   Greening Government 2003, HC 961

2001-02 Session

First   Departmental Responsibilities for Sustainable Development, HC 326
     (*Reply, Cm 5519*)
Second   Pre-Budget Report 2001: *A New Agenda?*, HC 363 (*HC 1000*)
Third   UK Preparations for the World Summit on Sustainable
     Development, HC 616 (*Reply, Cm 5558*)
Fourth   Measuring the Quality of Life: The Sustainable Development
     Headline Indicators, HC 824 (*Reply, Cm 5650*)
Fifth   A Sustainable Energy Strategy? Renewables and the PIU Review, HC 582
     (*Reply, HC 471*)
Sixth   Buying Time for Forests: *Timber Trade and Public Procurement*, HC 792-I ,
     (*Reply, HC 909, Session 2002-03*)

2000-01 Session

First   Environmental Audit: *the first Parliament*, HC 67 (*Reply, Cm 5098*)
Second   The Pre-Budget Report 2000: *fuelling the debate*, HC 71 (*Reply
     HC 216, Session 2001-02*)

1999-2000 Session

First	EU Policy and the Environment: An Agenda for the Helsinki Summit, HC 44 (*Reply, HC 68*)
Second	World Trade and Sustainable Development: An Agenda for the Seattle Summit, HC 45 (Including the Government response to the First Report 1998-99: Multilateral Agreement on Investment, HC 58) (*Reply, HC 69*)
Third	Comprehensive Spending Review: Government response and follow-up, HC 233 (*Reply, HC 70, Session 2000-01*)
Fourth	The Pre-Budget Report 1999: pesticides, aggregates and the Climate Change Levy, HC 76
Fifth	The Greening Government Initiative: first annual report from the Green Ministers Committee 1998/99, HC 341
Sixth	Budget 2000 and the Environment etc., HC 404
Seventh	Water Prices and the Environment, HC 597 (*Reply, HC 290, Session 2000-01*)

1998-99 Session

First	The Multilateral Agreement on Investment, HC 58 (*Reply, HC 45, Session 1999-2000*)
Second	Climate Change: Government response and follow-up, HC 88
Third	The Comprehensive Spending Review and Public Service Agreements, HC 92 (*Reply, HC 233, Session 1999-2000*)
Fourth	The Pre-Budget Report 1998, HC 93
Fifth	GMOs and the Environment: Coordination of Government Policy, HC 384 (*Reply Cm 4528*)
Sixth	The Greening Government Initiative 1999, HC 426
Seventh	Energy Efficiency, HC 159 (*Reply, HC 571, Session 2000-01*)
Eighth	The Budget 1999: Environmental Implications, HC 326

1997-98 Session

First	The Pre-Budget Report, HC 547 (*Reply, HC 985*)
Second	The Greening Government Initiative, HC 517 (*Reply, HC 426, Session 1998-99*)
Third	The Pre-Budget Report: Government response and follow-up, HC 985
Fourth	Climate Change: UK Emission Reduction Targets and Audit Arrangements, HC 899 (*Reply, HC 88, Session 1998-99*)

Printed in the United Kingdom by The Stationery Office Limited
5/2004   964988   19585

ISBN 0-215-01704-8

9 780215 017048